SUPER 31

NITESH MORE

To all the people,

Whom I have met and I am going to meet because I believe, These are the super people's who are teaching me a lot.

THANK YOU VERY VERY MUCH.

Contents

Contents

Contents

SUPER 31

Nitesh More

Be better or be the same. Choice is yours. - Nitesh More ."

PAST has Hold.
PRESENT is Missing.
FUTURE is a Big.....?

WHO WILL THINK, IF YOU DO NOT THINK ABOUT YOURSELF?

Most of us, Living a life in a past because Past has hold us tightly. Present is missing and Future is a Big ....?

Who will think about yourself,

If you do not think about yourself ?

Who cares,

If you do not care about yourself ?

Why don't you forgive and move on in life ?

We got only one life.

Are we really enjoying ?

By crying, If you get happiness then keep on crying.

Life will not change until you change.

Don't you want to be better?

You are the creator of your life. No one else .

Be different or be the same. If you do not do anything today, don't expect....,tomorrow will be different.

Yesterday, Today, Tomorrow will be the same or you want changes in your life.

Think, Rethink and again Rethink because This is your life and You know better.

Super 31 book is made with 31 chapters which is giving an information about How we think and How it is affected.

One word has a power to change your life or destroy your life so be the driver of your brain.

Find a purpose of your life and Make your life more meaningful.

ONE

1. ONE LIFE

One life can give you everything or can destroy your everything.

What do you choose ?

I always do MISTAKES and I think, Everyone does the same.

I always WAIT for others because I think, They will come in my life.

I always HELP others because I think, They will help me in my trouble time.

They will Give me their time.

They will GUIDENCE me.

They will MOTIVATE me.

Today or Tomorrow,

They will definetely come but I forgotten

The BITTER TRUTH of life, My time is going and I am just waiting for others by wasting my time.

They will not come and the TRUTH is, They don't want to come.

I just wanted that Someone should come in my life and give me their hand but It never happened.

You know what, I was the one who used to give an EXECUSES but now, I came to know that by giving an excuses, I can't change my life at all.

I must know that I am the one who can motivate myself.

I must know that I am the one who can push myself

I must know that I am the one who can change my life, No one else because This is my life and I must change because I have only one life.

I must take a stand,

I will fall..

I will fall again...

I will fall again and again....

But I must find my path and I need to walk on that path which I have found for myself to reach my goal.

Living a life is simple but not easy. I should accept this bitter truth.

I always think so many things in my mind but those things never happened but one bitter truth is that I have only one life and My time is running fast for waiting others.

One life where I can prove myself

One life where I can achieve my dream.

I should not wait for others.

I should stop waisting my time.

I must work on myself to reach my goal.

No one knows, When good time will come but Everyone knows, If we try to change our life, We can change.

I must start working on myself to have a better life.

A dream which I see when I eat,

A dream which I see when I cry,

A dream which I see when I drink,

A dream which I see when I sleep,

I must take a responsibility. I must see my future because It is neccessary to see.

If I work hard to achieve my dream,

If I push myself to achieve my dream

If I fight with struggles,

If I believe in me,

If I believe in my dream,

No one can stop me to reach my dream.

Stop wasting your time and start working on your dream.

Your time is going and you need to run with time.

I have only one life and I want to make my life more beautiful.

ALWAYS REMEMBER

- I have only one life.

- I am the only one who can help myself.

- Live a life fully.

- Those peoples who put me in trouble for making me strong.

Question No - 1

There is no tomorrow,

What will you do?

TWO

FORGIVE ME

If you want to have a peaceful life, The best option is to forgive them and move on in life.

Forgive me is a very simple word but very hard to say because of our Ego and Attitude.

Why we must say this to have a better life ?

I would like to explain by a story.

Are you ready ?

Of Course, You are.

The story is that Once a teacher tells his students, If you hate someone....You should give them a name like Potato, Onion, Chilly, Corriander etc.

By hearing all that, The students started,

Laughing and started making a fun.

Teacher said, Listen to the story further...

The person to whom the name is given,

They will give it and the name which is kept will keep that thing in their school bag.

After listening this,

The entire class were silent . They were looking at each other.

Teacher said,

Suppose If my enemy is potato, then I have to keep potatoes in my school bag.

Suppose If my enemy is chilly, then I have to keep chillies in my school bag.

After listening this, Whole class in tension. All of them quiet.

" The silence like watching a horror movie "

After few seconds, One student daringly ask,

To the teacher, What will happen If we do this ?

The teacher said,

Think....what will happen ?

One student said, after few days...they will rot, deteriorate and smell will start coming.

The teacher said, Perfectly recognised.

But teacher, what did we learn from this ?

Teacher is looking at students with sweet smile and says,

Whatever,

Whoever,

With whom you also have enmity. Forgive him and Move on in life....not rotting like those potatoes and don't be bad like coriander.

When will you keep these things with you in your bag..., you are the only one who is hurting to yourself with all those stuff.

It is better that you appologies to them and live life happily.

After hearing all this,

All the students started clapping but there was a one student...who was still in confusion.

He asked to teacher...why are you telling all this to us ?

We are all children and we don't have any enmity with anyone.

The teacher calmed down for a while and went to that child and said,

The things that we learn in a school are only a few percentage beneficial for our future but the story I have told you..will be usefull throughout your life and with this..you will remain a good person in the society and will try to make others good.

The entire class started clapping.

After this class, The whole class have requested to the management that we should have a one subject in which, we keep getting an inspiring stories for our better future.

ALWAYS REMEMBER

- To make others happy.

- To apologies, Instead of waiting.

- Be good with others for no reason.

- Do not go with stress at work and do not come with stress at home.

Question No - 2

Can you please make a list of those Peoples, Whom you want to forgive..?

Try...you will feel much better.

THREE
OPPORTUNITY

Time is totally changed. We used to wait for opportunities but now, This is the time to create the opportunity.

Opportunity is a word for which, Peoples are waiting in the world.

I wish, I had this opportunity,

I wish, I had got the opportunity.

I wish, If that opportunity was mine...,

And all...opportunity, Opportunity and opportunity.

So today, I am writing an inspiring story of opportunity.

Once a candidate was giving an Interview. During the interview...He said that If I get this opportunity,

Every second...I will work hard

After hearing this, The interviewer said, OK .

We will give you a task , If you complete that task...You will get a job on a good package in our company.

The candidate was very happy. He asked, What is the task ? I am so excited to do that.

Interviewer said,

We will take you to a room. There are many blue pens in a room and one of them is black ink in a blue pen.

Your task is to find a blank ink pen but If you throw away that black ink pen then you can not take that thrown pen.

Interviewer said to him that We are looking entire task in a camera.

Candidate was very happy.

He took a notebook for tasting a blue ink pen and black ink pen.

He was sure that finally, He will get this job.

He is going to give a test.

The candidate opened the door and saw that the entire room was filled with pens.

After seeing this,

He was in tension but he did not quit. He started doing the task in the hopes that I do not want to let this opportunity go.

He kept picking up the pen and started writing it and then throwing.

He kept doing this.

Kept on doing...

And kept on doing.

First 3 hours,

Then 4 hours,

And while doing so...almost 8 hours done.

He continue doing but as time passing, He was not testing with that much heart as he was doing before.

After 11 hours,

Finally, He found that pen which has a black ink but unfortunately, He got a habit to test a pen and throwing it in other room, and soon after he realised that he has lost this opportunity.

Candidate was a silent. He closed his eyes.

Somewhere he felt that...

Why ?

How ?

And for what reason ?

Am I lost ?

Something was running in his mind. He get up and started walking to go home.

He was disappointed and wondering how such a big mistake was made...?

What do we learn from this story ?

We have also started to become a lazy because we do not respect our time.

We do not value our time.

Like that blue pen, You are wasting every second...When will that black ink second

Come, Which will give you a great opportunity but we are used to like that blue pen.

Every second teach us something,

Every person..

Every pain...

Every thoughts...

Every things...

And you even don't know, When that second will come that will change your life forever.

So respect every second.

So respect every person.

So respect every pain.

So respect every things.

Because the respect create the opportunities.

ALWAYS REMEMBER

- To create an opportunities.

- To find a solution, Instead of waiting.

- To learn from new things.

- To know the value of every second.

Question No - 3

Can you please stop thinking about those opportunities which you have lost .?

Instead of that, Start thinking of ideas to create the new opportunities for you.

FOUR

ACTION

Every action has an opposite reaction but right action reach you towards goal.

Take an action, Do not care about result.

Not taking any action is the sign of looser.

Action is such a word, It takes much courage to do that.

We think that I will do this and then my life will be like this.

After 10 years, I will be here in the future and I will be anyhow...we just keep on saying.

Do we really take an action to achieve that milestone or just our thoughts are running in our mind...?

Do we really imagine ?

Imagination is very easy but taking an action on that is very difficult.

I personally feel,

If you want to bring a changes in your life.

Take a first step.

Take an action and let me tell you. After that action, It becomes your habit and once become your habit, No one can stop you until you stop.

If you want to do any work. The first step is to take an action and I am sorry to say that, but we are lazy to do that.

May be, because of Fear.

Everyone knows,

If I take an action in my work, My work will be amazing but from where do I start ?

I will not do it today.

I will do it tomorrow.

We have a habit to put on tomorrow and I am sure, It will never happen.

So what to do ?

How do we start taking an action ?

We actually wait for perfection and that's why we take more time.

Perfection will never come until you start...How will you know whether It is right or wrong ?

For example,

Take any company in the world.

Was it successful for the first time ?

Company made the product, then change the product, again they made the product then again changes in the product.

I don't know, How many times...company have change the product.

You can say like improvement, Modified, adding new things in the product.

They keep on doing changes by taking an actions to bring a right product in the market.

If they wait for the perfect product, there would be no company.

You can take an example of scientist,

How many experiments,

How many days,

How many weeks,

How many months,

How many years,

No one knows, When they will get a success but they do not stop taking an action.

You have to take a first step, Even If it is a small step.

Why not first step ?

Definetely, You should take because that first step slowly slowly increase by second step and then third step and continues...

After few days, You will never look back because you got habit of taking an action.

It does not matter to you because you are not waiting for perfection but by taking an action, you are making things perfectly.

ALWAYS REMEMBER

- To take an action.

- To be fearless.

- Not to worry about results. Just keep on doing.

- To find a better solution for every situation to take an action.

Question No - 4

Do you remember your last action which made you proud of.... ?

If not, This is your time.

Take an action and make yourself proud.

FIVE

24 HOUR

Time is running fast.

It does matter that How do you use your 24 hours ?

Please rethink about next 24 hours.

Are we use our time properly or wasting our time ?

No one can know this better than yourself, and I want you to ask yourself for getting a fair answer.

A poor person has a 24 hours and a rich person also has a 24 hours but then why poor peoples are becoming more poor and why the rich are becoming more rich.

What is that one thing.... Which poor people do not know and rich people knows very well.

Everyone starts from zero and the law of success is the same for everyone.

Then why not everyone rich ?

Have you ever asked yourself about time ?

No ...Not at all. Right.

It's a free of cost so why should I ask ?

What do you do in 24 Hours?

What to do in 24 Hours ?

Do you have any goal for next 24 hours ?

If not, then who will change your life ?

Why someone will change your life ?

You are the only one on this planet who is going to change your life, No one else.

If you have any goal, then you will plan your schedule for those 24 hours properly.

The main priority is discipline because I believe, Nothing is possible without discipline.

For example,

Just imagine....You follow the schedule for next 24 hours but later that day, You have not followed.

Can you become a rich ?

Without your next day plan, Do not go to sleep...If you want to see a changes in your life.

The second thing is that You make a plan but not taking an action...can you bring a changes in your life ?

Making a plan is very easy but following a plan is very difficult. If everyone seems easy then anyone can/could do it.

Why legends invest their time?

Are they crazy ?

Most of the peoples are much expert to give an excuses like,

I was ill.

I was busy.

I had a problem.

I had a problem at home.

I will do tomorrow and so on...

A person who knows the value of 24 hours. He will never waste it. Time is changing but poor is living a same life because He does not know, What is happening in his life.?

He is just getting up in the morning. Wasting a time by watching a TV. Spending much more time on mobile and doing nothing.

Are you happy with such type of life ?

Is your family happy ?

Do you like to waste your time ?

Have you wanted such type of life ?

Don't you want changes in your life ?

The day, When you start asking a questions like this. You will use your 24 hours better.

Than before because at that time, You will know the value of every second...therefore questions yourself and write an answer to those questions about moving forward in life.

ALWAYS REMEMBER

- Have only 24 hours.

- Will not get another day.

- Do it now.

- Be in present.

Question No - 5

Can you just imagine that you got only 24 hours and in that, You have to fulfill your all wishes....?

What and How will you do ?

Do you have your wish list ?

SIX

BEING POSITIVE

Positive thinking always help us to find a solution. It give us happiness and confidence so always be positive.

Being positive is simple but not easy.

It is a very simple thing which you have to add in your daily life to keep yourself positive but not easy at all. The reason behind is, May be laziness or put on some other time and that other time never comes.

You know what,

A human needs to eat a food daily to keep him healthy. Similar like to keep yourself positive, You need to add daily positivity in your life.

Today, Everyone wants to be positive. This is a very good thing and for that,

Some people loves to read a motivational books.

Some people loves to watch motivational movies.

Some people loves to hearing inspirational stories.

Some people loves to hear a motivational audios and so many other sources to keep themselves positive.

I think and I believe..

The person can stay positive as long as he is reading a books, watching motivatioanal movies, hearing inspirational stories and so on...

If they follow this, What will happen ?

I would like to say in a simple language that as we eat daily foods so our body works.... In the same way, Our brain needs a good thoughts.

As long as you put good ideas...till then our brain will work well and it will keep you positive.

The day, When you leave...negative thoughts start coming in our brain.

The solution is very easy.

Can you forget to eat the food ?

No..

What will happen If brain gets good ideas ?

Being positive is good for you as well for others... who is surround to you.

Positive things make you strong.

You get joy.

You get energy.

You start loving your life more than before.

You get solutions.

Everything seems more interesting.

Staying positive is the only one thing that can keep you moving and It is very easy for you to have a better life.

Do not let the negativity spread to you.

Stay away from those who talk negative things and spreading negativity.

A simple formula of having a happy life is being a positive...that's it.

ALWAYS REMEMBER

- Be positive.

- Be humble.

- Be different.

- Be better than yesterday.

Question No - 6

Do you love what you do ?

If not, How can you be positive..?

Can you make a list of those things, It can be anything....which keeps you positive.

SEVEN

ANGER

By showing an anger, You are losing to yourself. This is the right time to forget the anger and hug to patience.

Anger, It looks like the name is filled with full of Jeaolosy, Violence, Ego.

Nobody likes anger. We are hurt by anger but still we get angry.

Why?

I think, Everyone knows the reason behind the anger.

May be,

Tension,

Frastration,

Depression

Or something else

An angry person loose himself by small things because of those things, People like to stay away from angry person.

Nowadays, Life is running fast so indirectly people are going away from each other.

What is the use of such anger..., in which your relations are ending.

First, we must know...Why anger comes ?

According to research, It has been told that an angry person create the problems and promots the problem himself and because of that, He/She is facing a more trouble in their's life.

Do we need to be angry ?

Moreover, It was also said that We get angry on those peoples whom we want ..?

Whom we love...?

Somewhere angry people gives a hint to them that I am fed up with my life.

I need love.

I want to share something with you.

Someone should understand my problem.

Why I am behaving like this?

In the reality, It happens opposite. Whenever we get angry, the person in front feels so bad. He/She even does not try to understand.

It hurts their ego.

It hurts their attitude.

It hurts their behaviour.

It hurts their respect.

People stay away from that person and this is really worst part of our life.

May be, you are doing right but then why don't you think opposite?

If I were his/her place ...

Can't you even think about the problem ?

Is anything going wrong ?

After some time,

You can say Thank you by messaging or calling or mailing to that person, I am happy that your anger turned out on me and It proved to me that I have some place in your life.

By reading that message, angry person will start thinking that I have forgotten to live a life ?

Am I running away from my responsibilities ?

What happened is happened but by thinking about that, You are spoiling your present and when you spoil your present..., How can you make a better future ?

We all know that anger is dangerous for us so why do again, again and again ??

Is there anyone trying to control me ?

Am I someone's puppet ?

Those questions will automatically give the answer to angry person.

After this, Angry person will try to treat with others politely.

ALWAYS REMEMBER

- Keep the patience.

- Stay away from negative peoples.

- When you feel, Anger is coming..try to keep yourself busy in other stuff.

- Remember the best moments of life.

Question No - 7

Have you ever seen your video of anger ?

Just imagine.....

If you are true to yourself, You will get a clear picture.

EIGHT
NO EXCUSES

Excuses can help you for a sometime but the fact is, It is ruining your life and you are responsible for that. Try to understand this as soon as possible and stop giving an excuses.

No excuses means No excuses.

By giving excuses, You are lying to yourself. We have a habit to give a bullshit excuses, Instead of taking an action.

It is very simple to give excuses but very hard to live a life by excuses. You feel that I get happiness but the truth is, You are putting yourself in the problems.

Sometimes telling to peoples different stories like....

I am sad.

I have no money.

I do not get sleep.

I am facing so many problems.

I have a tension of....

I can not do this.

I do not have interest.

I have a problems with them and so on...

If you have a problem, who called it ?

You must accept this truth that you are the problem of your life and you are the solution of your life.

In this world, No one come to you for your benefit. Everyone come for their benefit and the main problem is you.

If you don't do something today, Nothing will be good. The saddest part is no difference between today and tomorrow.

A human wants to live a life in a past and that's the biggest excuses we have.

When you stop giving an excuses, that's the only day... You start loving your life. You start loving your work. You start loving what you love to do.

Everyone has a something unique to create an opportunity for themselves but we always choose giving excuses. We always put on next day, Your own skill create an opportunities for you.

Today is the only day which can bring a better tomorrow. If you wait for tomorrow, Things will not come to you.

We always like the life of those people who have everything.

Do you know how hard they have worked ?

Do you know how struggle they have done ?

Do you know how bad experience they have seen...but they never give an excuses. They started to working on their own.

They believed on themselves that tomorrow will be better.

This is the right time to stop giving an excuses and start working on yourself.

ALWAYS REMEMBER

- Winner find a solution.

- Never give up.

- Do it until you die.

- If not now then when ?

Question No - 8

Could you please make a list of your lovely excuses ?

If done, Read it again...

Have you found any of those excuses beneficial to your life ?

NINE

DO OR DIE

We are in this world to do something different but after coming in this world. We are not ready to face the struggle. We are running from problems.

It is very simple that If you want a better future then be ready for do and die.

If we do nothing today, Tomorrow we are going to die like this.

Everyone knows,

What to do ?

How to do ?

What is right ?

What is wrong ?

But we don't do because we have a habit to live a life like this.

If you want to do something, Get up and

Start working to make your own life. This is your life and you can change your life as you want. Just one thing is needed and that is dare to do something.

The spirit of doing something is courage.

You only have today, who always says..do. Do something because you have been sent to do something different in this world.

You can also make a history. To make a history...you have to live a life like do or die.

Today's world, People are running after each other. He/She is doing then I also follow him/her.

You should always do, what you love to do. It does not matter, What others are doing...that's not your path. Your path should be different than others to bring a changes in your life. Changes in society that's what, You are in this world.

What makes you different ?

What is your interest ?

If you start working on your interest which you love to do. No one can stop you to achieve what you have dreamed.

Day by day, working on your interest... you become stronger than before. Your future is in your hand so make it inspiring or leave it dying.

ALWAYS REMEMBER

- Just do it. Don't think much.

- Be ready for falling again and again.

- Either you will win or you will get a lesson.

- Before dying, make a name.

Question No - 9

What is your life after death ?

Do you want that people should know you before and after the death ?

If yes,

Be ready for do or die.

TEN

WALK ALONE

Instead of walking with others, Walk alone. You do not need any permission to walk alone. Walking alone makes you strong. It gives a power and strength.

Just walk alone.

Do not stop.

Do not see back.

Just walk.

Today, we are talking about those people who walked alone because they believed in themselves that walking alone means becoming strong.

Taking one step towards success.

Are you ready to walk alone?

Do you need support from someone?

There is no need to wait for a single person nor to take anyone's permission to walk alone.

You can see/read a history of those who walked alone are the most successful because they found their own way.

They believed, Every problem has a solutions.

So why wait for ..?

They walked,

They fallen,

They walked again...

They fallen again...

They kept walking...

They kept faling...but they do not stopped walking.

Every time after falling, there was the energy to rise again.

Those people, Who walk alone knows that

If shadow also leaves then why take support from someone else ?

They have learned that to live in this world, you have to help yourself by yourself because as long as you are rich, as long as you are good, as long as your feet move, people will come to you.

After that, What to do ?

If you are depend on someone...

There will be a lot of darkness in life, but after every darkness, second day comes then why do we afraid to walk alone..?

Why wait for someone ?

Why take someone's support ?

Why take someone's permission ?

Why spread your hand in front of someone ?

You are on this planet to fly. By slowly, slowly... you will also fly. Everyone's time come so...your time also will come.

Don't wait for the opportunity. You are here.

To create the opportunity by taking small steps, so just walk alone and do not depend on anyone for help because If you can't help to yourself then why do you expect from others to help you. If you can't take a stand to improve your life then why do you expect from others to improve you.

You are the only one, who wash your own ass. Do not depend on someone to come and wash your ass.

ALWAYS REMEMBER

- **Walk alone for being strong.**

- **Walking will teach you running.**

- **Be independent.**

- **Be better.**

Question No - 10

What is stopping you by walking alone ?

Do you expect that someone should walk with you ?

Why ?

ELEVEN
QUITTING

Loser only quit. Winner's always find a solution to get up. If quitting is the last option then why did you start ? Always keep in mind that Quitting is not the solution.

We always have a two options.

Either we should quit or we should catch. It depends on the situation but quitting is always wrong.

You should always remember one thing in life and that is, If I wanted to quit then why I started ?

Why I dream, When I have to quit...

Why I don't sleep, When I have to quit...

Why I believe, When I have to quit...

Quitting is very easy.

Next second, and you quit but how much time we took to start the same thing...?

We think so many times before starting.

We understand so many times before starting.

We dream so many times before starting.

We ask so many times before starting.

After so much of time wasting,

Finally we decide to do it and after one bad incident, After one mistake, After one wrong way...We feel to quit because quitting is very simple and easy.

Falling is very easy but getting up is very hard.

Right ?

You have to quit because you are tired.

You have to quit because your trust is broken.

You have to quit because you are hurt.

You have to quit because no one cares.

If you quit today, You will never catch it again. Better think about it.

I know, you are suffering but quitting is not a solution. Suffer little more and enjoy your success.

Those people are always respected who has made it. Their status tells everything. You want to be one of them. Think once again before quitting.

People will tell your name as an inspiration or people will tell your name as a loser.

You better know, which one suits to you.

The world will recognize you by your work, by your story, by your status, by your behaviour,by your biography etc etc.

Today's your pain is the light of your tomorrow.

When you feel like quitting...ask yourself one question? Why I started ?

ALWAYS REMEMBER

- Quitting is like dying.

- Quitting is not the solution.

- Loser quits. Are you ?

- So many solutions are there

Question No - 11

If you are going to quit, better do not start.

Rethink before quitting.

Why I started ? If I wanted to quit...

Instead of quitting,

Could you please find a solution ?

TWELVE
STRUGGLE

Struggle has to be there in our life for better experience. If you get a success without struggle, there is no value of that success.

Without struggle, Life is nothing. Struggle is like a gift in our life.

A struggle is the only thing that helps a person to become a powerful.

Life is a struggle and struggle is a key to success.

There is an infinite tragedy in life that a person who gets a success early...does not have a long holiday and the person who moves forward by struggling always has a success.

There is a one problem in some people. They keep struggling and then halfway the leave.

I think, no person can go ahead without struggle because the person who sees the struggle will have a solution for everything.

Life is equal to struggle.

Struggle helps to make you a successful person.

Struggle helps to make you a strong person.

Struggle helps you to make work hard.

Struggle gives a different experience of life.

Life without struggle means the days are coming and going. Nothing else is happening.

If you want to reach your goal then be ready for struggle and If you are ready for struggle then be ready to success. It is as simple as that.

Life is to be lived...

Do not just live, but live the life of such a person who welcomes every struggle as a gift.

Who are you ?

What do you do ?

How do you do ?

How world will know ?

If you struggle then your story will know.

Who you are....

What you did....

How you did....

What happened in past....

How was your journey...

From now, welcome struggle as a gift and make your life so beautiful.

One day, When you will see in a past. You will see an inspiring journey of struggling days.

People will see your biopic. You never know anything can happen in this world.

Miracles happen but not in a one night so always be ready for struggle as a learner.

One day, people will be waiting for the interview because you have done it. You inspired others by your struggling journey.

Everyone wants to become a model but I say, Instead of becoming a model...be a role model of someone.

What do you say ?

Always keep in mind, Struggle is a gift and I welcome to struggle.

ALWAYS REMEMBER

- Be ready for struggle.

- Be ready for hard work.

- Be ready to face the challenges.

-Struggle now and enjoy the success later.

Question No - 12

Have you really faced the struggle ?

Just for a few second, Can you imagine of those peoples who does not have an Eyes, Legs, Hands, ETC ?

THIRTEEN
DIFFICULTIES

Everyone feels difficulties because it is a part of our life but how we face the difficulties, can make a big differences.

Welcome to difficulties because difficulties are the part of our life.

Difficulties are blessings, If you are facing.

Difficulties are opportunities for us.

Difficulties works as a pearls in our life that's why I say, Welcome difficulties.

If you have difficulties in your life. You are at right path to reach your goal.

The day, When difficulties stop coming in your life. You are indirectly stopping yourself from growths.

To grow a person, challenges are very important. Difficulties help to make a human being a very powerful.

The way, we welcome our guest... the same way, we must welcome difficulties..if you want to get ahead in life.

Face the difficulties,

When you face your difficulties in peace, difficulties will start running away from you because your calm behaiour, because you welcome them as an experience.

You have got the habit of welcoming them with love.

When you face difficulties, your intension of looking at difficulties are completely changed.

You also get power from difficulties and the same can be taken also If run from them.

One thing always to remember is that difficulties are there for a some time in our life and the second thing is that difficulties come to teach something to move on.

You can not avoid difficulties but you can drive away difficulties by welcoming them.

Keep in mind and welcome difficulties with smile and love.

ALWAYS REMEMBER

- Welcome difficulties

- Face the difficulties with smile.

- Difficulties comes for better growths.

- Life has no value, If there are no difficulties.

Question No - 13

Do you have any list of your difficulties ?

Be better by facing every difficult situation.

FOURTEEN

CRY

Crying can make you strong or even weak. It is our emotions that to bring outside or hide inside

Crying is best when you are in darkness.

People go to the bathroom and cry whenever they are sad....,

But

But when they come out, they come with hopes that It will not happen again.

Sometimes after crying, feels strong.

If crying is the solution to anything , then every human being succeeds.

What is the meaning of cry, If there is no anger.

If you want to cry,

When you wake up, cry

When you go, cry

When you think, cry

By crying, If you make a history then please cry loudly. The world should know this formula of being happy, being succeeds.

What is the need to cry ?

It is said that bad days comes in our life to have a good days but to have a good days, you need to face a so many things.

You must learn to fight to make your dreams come true.

One boy always used to cry.

One day, he went to the monk and said, I want to be rich. I do not like my life at all.

What should I do to be happy ?

The monk said, can you do as I say ?

Boy replied, Yes.

The monk started saying that..., please go to the some railway stations and do the observations.

Go to some signals and do the observations.

Once you finish that come to me.

The boy did all that what monk has said. Coming return to monk...but this time, his attitude was completely changed because he did an observation at the station and at the signal that he had never tried to understand.

We also see those things but we are still unknown because we are running in life and nobody knows, why are we running away ?

The question is, What he observed ?

There were so many beggars at the stations.

Some without hand,

Some without leg,

Some without eyes,

Children's are begging.

Slept on road.

Dirty clothes

Food which is smelling.

Not bathing from how many days...

Their own shit is nearby.

The boy walked through the gate and felt, If I always cry for small things then that day is not far away to be like one of them.

Everybody knows,

If someone takes care of someone, then someone else will take care of someone.

The law of nature says, What goes around that's come around.

The boy understand the reality of life.

After this, he started learning. He started observing. He started enjoying. He started being happy

You know what, crying make us weak but If you are happy by crying then keep on crying.

If you get love by crying then keep on crying.

If you get to learn from crying then keep on crying.

If you get anything from crying then keep on crying but remember one thing always that crying is not the solution for anything.

Crying plays a role with emotions. When crying will be done. Stop crying and start doing because If you do something, you will definitely get something, but If you keep on crying then you will only waste your time, energy which is not good at all.

Stop crying and start working on yourself to bring a changes in your life because you are the creator of your life.

Don't destroy by crying for small stuffs and making things more complicated.

Emotions are good for observation but being practical is much more important as well.

ALWAYS REMEMBER

- Do not cry for small things.

- Makes you weak.

- Sometimes it is good but not all time.

- Do not go in past and then start crying.

Question No - 14

What is that one thing which bring a smile on your face..?

Who is that special one who does not want to see you crying...?

FIFTEEN
BURDEN

Why ?

Who said to take the burden ?

It is killing our present.

Be a burden free please.

Can anyone become a successful with a burden ?

Burden gives a stress in our life.

If you want to get rid of it, leave them and move on in life.

If you are living with burden, you are spoiling your life along with family.

Because of burden...you can not be happy.

No one can be happy with you because you.

Have taken so much of burden seriously.

The best way is to leave a burden where it is and start working on something which gives you a happiness.

Nowadays, Every person is sick from burden because they are taking a burden for small things.

Is it really necessary ?

Leave where it is and move on...It is as simple as that.

Someone said something, you started taking a burden.

Someone said something, you started showing an anger.

By taking a burden, you are just destroying. Nothing else is happening. You can not do anything new with burden.

If someone give something to others, you started thinking about that.

Why ?

Burden can make you sick. It can mentally attack.

There are so many such a stories about depression.

Why all those happened..?

It is all happening because you are taking a burden.

Forget about it. Whatever happened is happened but because of that, why do you take a burden ?

With burden, you can not have a happy life.

If you want to be good with yourself, with everybody....live freely.

It does not matter what others are thinking and If it matters then you are not living your life because your control is in someone's hand.

Better you should think about it and start living a peaceful life.

ALWAYS REMEMBER

- Leave the burden where it is.

- Be free.

- Enjoy today.

- Feel the power of now, instead of taking a burden.

Question No - 15

Can you please sit at one place for a long time ?

Just imagine ?

For how long ?

Even you can't sit at one place and have a relaxation.

Then why do you take a burden..? and What is your burden ?

Be burden free and enjoy.

SIXTEEN

RISK

Leaders only take a risk. Are you a leader? If not.., time to think about it. Life is all about risk. Take a risk and enjoy the sweetness or keep sitting. Actually, Who cares...?

The lot of people are scared of the risk word because it feels a person that it will put in a big problem.

If you want to move forward in your life. It is very important to take a risk because If you do not take any risk, then how will you know whether it is right or wrong.

If you want to grow in your life. Start taking a risk. It can put you down but for sure, It will bring you up to grow and that's the simple formula of risk.

Risk acts like a hope in our life.

Most people play for a safety and this is the most useless thing we do.

Actually, we have a habit of hiding from taking a risk.

If you want to play, play freely. It will help you in the field.

It is very easy to leave the field but it is very difficult to stay in the ground.

If life is like a field...,

When you play freely, then see what the ground does for you.

Suppose you are playing a match and you are a bowler. You just keep hoping that I just want to finish my over...without giving more runs or If you want to give at least minimum runs, then you will only keep bowl away from the batsman. Just for hiding because you are not taking the risk to take the wickets and when you put the ball to take the wickets, May be...your every ball will be 4 or

6 but this is the one thing that will help you to take the wickets...so it is also a risk.

You have to understand the game of risk and then take the risk to take the wickets.

If you want to escape then stay away from the field. Just watch the match from outside.

It does not matter,

What are you doing....but when it matters, You do make a difference because this is your life and you have to make your life awesome because this is your life, No one else.

If you want to be better,

It is very important to take a risk and always keep in mind that too much of thinking about risk, will kill your goal.

ALWAYS REMEMBER

- Not taking any risk, that is also a big risk.

- Risk is a part of life. Must face.

- Be better by taking a risk or be same.

- Risk is like a hope.

Question No - 16

What is that, Which is stopping you to take a risk...?

Be the same or be the change by taking a risk.

SEVENTEEN
PERSISTENCE

Being persistence is always helpful because it gives a strengths for better tomorrow.

The person who has a habit of persistence, he will never fail in life.

In a simple language, It is an ability that sets you apart from others, When the rest of the players leave, but you keep standing....this is called persistence and this is the only one quality that leads you to success.

Make yourself so capable in life so that there will be no situation of falling down again and again and again and If it's happening then you have a solution of being persistence.

When others trying to give up in the world. You have to stand and say loudly, take my test, I am ready for it.

If I fail, I will try once again until I succeed.

I am ready to face the good and bad time because I never give up.

There is no place for giving up in life, If you want to be successful.

Do not worry about opportunities because opportunities will come and go but If there is persistence, you will create more opportunities for you.

You will also show the world that What are you and what the soil, you are made of....

Make a plan,

Take an action.

Take an action again,,,

Keep doing this until you reach your destination.

It is very easy to give up but the give up is not made for you and It was never made for you.

May be, your plan will not work...

May be, you are struggling... but if you want to get a success. You have to hug the failure and this is what makes a different from others.

Do you know ?

After every failure, You become stronger.

(sometimes, It can be opposite...if you think in a negative way...)

Every failure,

Your intension is to reach the destination becomes stronger.

We fail, when we stop doing.

You are the magic of your goal and your goal is waiting for you.

Why should you not leave the half way?

We must keep going until achieve the dream.

No situation is a big or small. It just, how we think and how we solve that's it. Similar like, no dream is a small or a big dream until you think about your dream and how you make a plan to reach your dream.

ALWAYS REMEMBER

- Be persistence.

- Keep this quality with you. You will never fail.

- Good for better tomorrow.

- Be consistence, persistence will follow you.

Question No - 17

Persistence is the only key to success.

You are the key of your life.

Have you still locked yourself from discovering ?

Whom you are waiting to open that lock ?

EIGHTEEN

YOU

You are the creator of your life and you are the one, who only destroy.

Who you wanna be ?

Nothing will change until you change. You are the one who is responsible for everything.

Do you give credit to others, If something happens good with you...???

Do you blame to others when something happens wrong with you...?

(you know this better)

As long as you do not accept this reality, You will remain the same because you were doing the same yesterday and even today

And you are going to stay the same tomorrow.

If you want some changes in you, then first change to yourself.

As soon as you change, things will change automatically and If things change then improvement will come and If the improvement comes then nothing can stop you from getting a success because you are the architech of your life.

Everything you need to gain.

Success is within you, you just have to get those things out. If you can not do, you are only responsible, no one else.

If you do not change now, you can not change anything.

Nobody knows, when god will call ? but until you live

Why not make your dreams come true ?

Why not live a happy life...

Why not live life completely...

If the death comes, you should happily hug. This will happen If you have achieved what you wanted to achieve.., otherwise after death also, you won't be happy.

Everyone knows,

Time is getting shorter, then why not change yourself from now...this is that moment.

Why not take the pledge to change yourself?

Don't you love your dream ?

Are you used to being lazy ?

Are you known as a looser ?

Today is the time that you can change yourself .

Your thinking....

Your attitude....

You can make yourself a better person.

For sure, this will happen when you feel to change yourself.

Hey, Why did you come in this world ?

Hey, What did you give to this world ?

If you want to give, then first you give to the world then this world will give you more than enough.

Your life is in your hands.

Your dreams are in your hands.

Your happiness is in your hand.

Your moment is in your hand.

Everything is with you but you are finding somewhere else.

You are not at present.

Why do you feel tired because of loosing something.

To be frank,

you have already lost so many things.

It is a time of getting up.

You have those abilities to change the world but first, you have to change yourself.

Be better than yesterday to have a better tomorrow.

ALWAYS REMEMBER

- You only matters, No one else.

- Right or wrong. You better know.

- You only create or destroy.

- Be true to yourself because It's you.

Question No - 18

You have come this world without bringing anything.

From then...

You got so many things. It means, you are in profit.

So why do you afraid of loosing anything ...?

Make a list of loosing things ?

If you loose..., nothing will happen.

Either you can win or learn a lesson.

NINETEEN

WHO AM I ?

Do you have any answer for this ?

If yes, It means, you have made it.

If not, start working to show the world.

Who am I ?

Do you have any respect in this world ?

Do I live happily ?

Am I someone ?

I am just going into the crowd where no one belongs to anyone.

Everyone is there, just to say but really everyone is there for you.

When the time comes, everyone is outspoken.

Then who am I ?

Am I same like them ?

Don't I have any value ?

The value will be created when you do something. Something different. Something better. Something to bring a changes. It is you who have to create your own value to bring a changes.

There is no one and no one will come. If I live a life like this.

Life is easy to live but we have never learned to live.

We are taught to suffer.

We are taught to follow.

We are just running away.

From how many days,

From how many weeks,

From how many months,

From how many years,

And even don't know...why we are running.?

Others are running that's why, we are also running.

Have you ever asked ?

Who am I ?

Why am I running ?

Why am I doing ?

The answer will be anything...

I am lost.

I am tired.

I am scared.

I have a dram but unable to do anything because of,,,,

No idea.

And I am blaming someone else for this.

Who are those?

What is their mistake ?

Why am I behaving like this ?

Why is not happening as I had planned ?

Do I really want this type of life ?

Have you ever imagined of this by asking a question to yourself?

We love to ask a questions to others, but never ask questions to ourself because we are afraid to face the truth.

You and your dreams has a only one wall and that's you. You have to remove/break that wall to find the real purpose to live a life.

To create a life is in my hand and similarly, ruining a life is in also my hands.

It is me who never learned to loose because when I loose, I also learn something.

People will say anything behind but I am the hero of my life.

When I start to bring the changes,

I will fall,

I will fall again,

I will fall thousand times,

But I will rise again because fight is in my blood.

I am a warrior and I am always ready to rise.

I am what I am.

I am the change of my life and that is my identity.

<u>ALWAYS REMEMBER</u>

- Am I exit in this world ?

- Look at yourself.

- Why are you in this world ?

- What makes you different than others...?

Question No - 19

Have you ever asked to yourself,

Who am I ?

Instead of finding an answers, Ask questions to yourself because we have a habit of asking questions to others.

TWENTY
GIVING

If you want a satisfaction in your life, then start giving.

Giving is the best communication in our life.

By giving something, small or big, It feels great. Feels happiness. Feels satisfaction and trully, get a good sleep in night.

A smile on someone face make us more satisfied.

By heart, you should try at least, you will come to know the satisfaction of giving to others.

If you give something today, you will get something better tomorrow.

Do not expect anything from anyone because giving is like taking and when we started to expecting...it kills our joy.

There are so many successful people in this world but before becoming a success,

Did they know the formula of success?

Did they have a name in the market ?

Was success in their blood?

Not at all...,

They gave first and then after so many years they get because they knew the value of giving.

Giving can be anything.

Someone gave their time.

Someone worked hard by giving much attention to work.

Whenever they lost,

They stood up because they knew the value of giving.

Whenever opportunity comes, they tried to grab it because they were ready to give their time, their hard work to get a success.

Those who are succeeded because they had a faith in themselves that I can do this and I am going to get back more than what I am giving today.

They believed in themselves.

The law of success says,

When any person ready to put himself with full faith and dedication...success is attracted towards them.

This is a life like giving and taking.

Give what you have to get a success and celebrate your success after some year because It is a process of making you more stronger, more attractive, more understanding, more interesting, more Experience in the field where you love to do.

Never work, If you don't like that work.

Work there, where you love to do that work otherwise you will waste everything.

Always do your best and give more than you take.

Just think, If anyone says to you...

What will you do for your company ?

What can you do after hearing this ?

If he/She does not have the heart to give anything to his/her work ,

How will that person progress?

Whatever field it is,

Unless you show extraordinary additional skills then how can you be different from others?

If you do not try to improve your performance, what do you expect ?

Success or failure,

I think, you better know.

Have you seen any sports person or try to observe them ?

They keep believing that practice is something that can make them better than yesterday.

They do not see day,

They do not see night,

They just keep on practising for improvement.

Their only motive remains that, first i have to do something which I have to pay to get the medal. Rest will come later.

After getting a medal also, they keep on practising.

Always remember, First you sow and then you reap.

Just give it, Success is yours.

ALWAYS REMEMBER

- Give without expectation.

- Giving is a sign of good human being.

- Giving is a best communication.

- Just give by heart.

Question No - 20

Would you like to be the smile of someone ?

just do it.

The satisfaction of giving is an amazing.

TWENTY-ONE

FEAR

Fear is nothing. It is our brain popping. Winner does not care about fear and I am sure, You are a winner.

Fear is a motivation for the person who wants to make a victory.

Why are we afraid ?

Are we afraid of our dreams?

Is our mind afraid of fear ?

Do we take a fear very seriously ?

Does our inner strength afraid of fear?

Fear is nothing. It just a feeling comes in us that creates the fear.

Do not be afraid of fear, Instead of face it.

Actually, fear is not what we think,

Fear is like If I fail, people will laugh at me. I am afraid of how I will go in front of others.

How will I face them?

You know, what is right for you but because of fear, You do not take any action.

When you face the fear, you learn to fight yourself.

If you are afraid of fear, you will remain the same and If you remain the same then you will not be anywhere. It just days are coming in your life and you are just wasting by yourself.

Keep walking in life, If you want to have a better life.

If you want to have a rest, then no need to do anything.

A person who starts to walk, slowly, slowly...he/she starts to run.

Fear is the one that help us to reach our goal.

Fear is just a feeling.

Neither you can see it , nor you can touch it,

Why scared of fear ?

Fear will not come until you give a permission to come in. It is your decision to follow the fear or face the fear.

If you beat your fear, then you win. If you don't then you loose.

You must remove the fear word from your dictionery, from your mind, from your blood, from your body and replace with success.

For some people, the act of fear is a motivation and for some people....it is a demotivation.

Depends on... how you take it.

Failure are those peoples, who have a fear of starting.

If you want to do something different in life, do not afraid of fear... just face it.

Make your fear as your power.

It is not written anywhere that you can fail, so do not afraid of fear but start with fear as a strength.

ALWAYS REMEMBER

- Kill your fear before it kills you.

- Face it with smile.

- Can fear give you in written that you will fail..?

- You have abilities to face the fear.

Question No - 21

Fear is something that has hold you from last how many years ?

This is the right time to face the fear and be different than others.

Could you please make the list of your fears ?

because the answer is within.

TWENTY-TWO
DECISION

Decision can be right or wrong but not taking a decision is always wrong. Take a decision and see the result.

Most successful people in this world have a unique quality..., that is the decision making because this is the only thing that decides to take an action.

By taking a decision, you get the energy to work better than before.

People who can not take a decision can never become a successful because to get a success, one must have a quality of taking a decision.

Waiting is good but for how long ?

One day, you have to have a decision... without that, how will you know ?

Was that a right or wrong decision ?

This is the one bad thing that we do afraid of taking a decision.

It is not necessary that every decision will be right, but If you do not take the decision then how will you take an action ?

The sooner, you take a decision...the better it becomes...but remember that you are not taking a decision in a hurry.

A thought can never be right without thinking.

You have to take a quick decision because ideas can come in anyone's mind.

May be, you are wasting to take a decision and other side, someone else started.

No situation is a right or wrong.

The situation can be very good and it can give you more benefit but other side, it can be worst... but sometimes, somewhere, you have to take a decision to be a successful person.

The habit of successful people is, they take quick and quality decision and because of, they are a different from others.

Why we afraid to take a decision ?

Why we are unable to take a decision because we are afraid that If the decision becomes wrong then It can put us in a trouble.

May be, this is the fear we have of not taking a decision but can you live a better life ?

Can you give a better life to family ?

Can you live happily ?

I must say, you should ask this type of questions to yourself because It can help you to have a better life.

Better than yesterday.

Better than today.

Fear never lets a person to take a decision .

What will happen ?

That's the one thing has hold you from taking a decision.

ALWAYS REMEMBER

- Take a quick decision.

- Understand the value of quick decision.

- Think , think again and take a decision but quickly.

- Who can take the decision of your life.?

Question No - 22

Do you remember your last decision ?

I guess,

You do not remember because you have still not taken any decision.

TWENTY-THREE

PERFECTION

No one is a perfect and not any situation is a perfect situation. You can make it perfect by improving yourself. So are you ready for improvement ?

The bitter truth of life..., If you wait for the perfection in your life, you will never be able to do anything in your life because things or situations are never perfect and never will be perfect.

The person has to make those things perfect.

I have seen so many peoples who used to say that we will start working, when things will be good.

They are still starting and it will never happen.

Do you know ?

You are made for perfection.

Sadly, you never understand this.

What is a human ?

A human is a person, who can do anything possible. He has abilities to make things happen.

When you start working on yourself , you will come to know ...,

What are you ?

Who are you ?

What can you do ?

What is your limit ?

It will happen when you start thinking about yourself.

When you start improving yourself.

Only those people knows, this bitter truth when they start working on themselves.

Today, may be..you are not in good condition but you want to make a good condition.

But how will this happen ?

No one knows,

Only you know yourself better than anyone.

You know your limitations.

You are the creator of your life.

Everything happens,

You are the responsible for what is happening with you.

If you are not thinking about yourself then who will think about you.?

Who has a time to think about you ?

Who wants to see you better ?

Is there anyone ?

If someone is there for you then I must say, you are the lucky one on this planet. At least, people think about you.

In other situation, you have to think about yourself anyhow. No other choice at all.

If you are still waiting for better situation then I must say, you are wasting your time, energy.

Slowly, you are ruining your life.

Better do not wait for perfection.

Just start doing because this is only way that leads you to perfection.

Whatever you have...

Wherever you are..

It does not matter.

Just do it and If you really want to wait for the perfection,

Read it very carefully and understand it very very carefully.

Think like,

This is the last job of your life or

This is the last client of your life.

After this,

You will not get any job, project, client,

In this situation,

What will you do ?

Please do ask yourself for better answer because you know yourself better than anyone.

No one is stopping you. You are the only one who has stopped yourself.

ALWAYS REMEMBER

- Do not wait for perfection.

- Ready for improvement.

- No situation is a perfect situation.

- Think out of the box to make a situation perfectly.

Question No - 23

Are you waiting for perfection ?

If yes,

Why ?

Keep on waiting. Nothing will change.

No one is perfect, then how can you be perfect ?

TWENTY-FOUR

PAIN

Without pain, life is nothing. If anyone says, I don't have any pain or I have not seen any pain in my life. It means, they have not seen the life. Pain is must in our life. Pain can take you to reach our goal.

Always keep in mind that pain is temporary.

If there is no pain in life, you will never understand the good and bad experience of life, so pain is must in our life.

Every person should thank to pain because pain give us so many lessons to understand life better.

What is the meaning of our life ?

Why are we on this planet ?

If you feel pain, others also feel pain. If there is no pain in life, you would never get up in life and you will be always there where you used to be.

People lost their money, they feel the pain.

People lost their girlfriend, they feel the pain.

People lost their equipments, they feel the pain.

People lost their loved one, they feel the pain.

People have lost so many things and because of that, they have changed the way of looking at life.

Peoples have become more successful because of pain.

A person who does not feel the pain or have not seen the pain in his life, he has not experienced the life yet.

He/she needs to see so many things.

He/she needs to understand so many things.

He/she needs to learn so many things.

He/she needs to observe so many things.

Why do bad things happen to good people?

Why goodness is a bad thing.

Whenever there is a big tragedy happens with us,

We say,

I wish...I had known.

I wish....someone had spoken.

Why our tomorrow is most important than today because It says, feels the pain today.

And eat the sweetness tomorrow.

The more you feel the pain today,

The more you will fail,

If you want to get out of it,

Then learn from that and move forward in life because This is your life.

ALWAYS REMEMBER

- **Feel the pain.**

- **Pain is a key to success.**

- **Pain today, enjoy tomorrow.**

- **Pain can kill you or teach you. Choice is yours..?**

Question No - 24

What is your pain ?

You must think about it for your better future.

TWENTY-FIVE

PROBLEMS

Do not think much about problems. It is a something that gives a strength to solve the problem. Always remember that every problem has a solution and every solution has a problem.

When the problem come at you, you must congratulate to yourself.

You feel bad after hearing this but still I say the same.

If there is no problem, there is no solution. To get the better solution, you must face the problem with smile and congratulate yourself for facing the problem without fear.

For example,

There is a disease, there is a medicine as a solution.

There is a walking problem, there is a van as a solution.

There are so many things come in our life as a problems and we get a solution by facing the problem.

If we ignore the problem,

After some time, it will become a headache to you.

It is all happened because of those problems and problems are like an opportunities.

The problems come to those people who have an abilities to face it.

I wish, you could understand the importance of problems. It is a part of our life to make a better person.

If there is no problem, life is useless. There is no meaning to live a life, so welcome the problems with smile and congratulate to yourself.

Each and every person is struggling for something but not in a right way because they are running for something else.

When you think about solution, problem is nothing. It is just an experience to be a better.

For some people,

Problems become a big problems.

For some people,

Problems become an opportunity.

It is depend on our thinking.

How we take that problem ?

Always remember, you are a fighter and you have the ability to solve the problem.

Have you ever thoughts about it ?

When you focus on problems, you create more problems but when you focus on

Solutions, you create more opportunities.

Always do one thing, If problems come...

Understand the problem carefully and then start finding a solution.

Most of the time, we find a solution first and then try to understand the problem.

There is a power in us that we can do anything.

If we think, we can then definitely we can.

Just congratulate the problem and welcome them in your life.

ALWAYS REMEMBER

- Problems for better future.

- Every problem has a solution.

- Feel the experience of problems.

- Face the problem or fear the problem.

Question No - 25

Problems come to those who have an abilities to solve it.

I am sure, you have that in built.

What's your problem ?

Have you still not solved ?

Solve it before becoming a burden.

TWENTY-SIX

COMFORT ZONE

Get out of it now because comfort zone make you lazy. If you want to be different then leave the comfort zone please.

The comfort zone is a disease and If it is found, you can not do anything because you like to live in the comfort zone.

I am telling you with the help of story. It will help you to better understand.

There was a family, having 2 boys.

After 24 hours,

Father said to them that from tomorrow, you have to report to the office because study is finished and this is the right time to learn about running a home bussiness.

Both said, yes.

In the morning, one of them refused to go to the office and this was happening again and again at home.

After few months,

The one who joined the office, was doing a very well and the one who refused to go. He got a bad habits of drinking an alcohol, smoking cigaretts etc etc

The father was in tension. He was not understanding. What to do ?

He called his friend and saying a bad habits about son.

What should I do ?

Friend gave an advise to him,

If you want to bring your son on a right track, you have to do one thing...

May be, you and your family won't like it but still I say this,

Entire family should shift to some other place and keep that son alone at home.

Give a paid holidays to your servant, who work in that house.

Let them enjoy.

Before leaving the house,

Do not keep anything at home.

Do not keep money at home.

Do not keep any eating material at home.

Do not keep any drinking materials.

After some time,

Father came at home and telling the plan for shifting and why is he doing ?

Everyone refused to do that but later on, they are ready for the son. They just want to try, If it can help.

According to their plan,

Everything was going right.

The son was also very happy at home because he got freedom to live a life.

Days were going.

After 25 days,

He came to know that his money is finished. He started to find at home. Everything he checked. Even twice checked the bank balance. He had finished all the money into alcohol, cigarette, online foods, casino and so on...

He was in tension. He was calling to friends for money but nowadays, who give money to drunk person.

Finally, he calls to family members for money.

Family member said that we are out of country.

After coming, we can give. This time not possible for us. We are also stuck here.

Actually, they lied.

He went to the office and asking to account manager for money but he also did not give because of permission.

He tried all the way to get the money but could not work.

He is remembering those moments when he had a money and how he wasted them.

He started crying but crying is not the solution for money.

He needs to earn the money.

Finally, he started to find a job because he had no other way.

At first,

He had difficulty to do a job but after sometime, he started doing a good.

When he came to know that all the roads are closed for him. He create a new door by finding a job and working their regularly for earning a money.

The moral of the story is,

If you get everything freely and easily, then you will always get the same way, which

Make you a more lazy person and you enter in a comfort zone which is really dangerous.

Those people, who live in the comfort zone can never work hard, can never struggle and can not do anything new in life.

ALWAYS REMEMBER

- Comfort zone is a disease.

- Get out of it as soon as possible.

- Better life or same life.

- Earn everything respectfully.

Question No - 26

Are you suffering by comfort zone disease ?

TWENTY-SEVEN

LAZINESS

Laziness can give a happiness for a sometime but it is destroying your life for lifetime.

The routine of living a life is totally changed and because of this, we have become a lazy and our laziness killing our life.

What is the reason ?

Let's start with the story to understand better about laziness.

One man was a very lazy. As day passing, his life was becoming more worst.

He was thinking.

Why is this happening ?

Have I done wrong with anybody?

Am I really bad ?

He was alone, so many thoughts was coming. It was making him disturb.

Tears started coming. He feels that angers but he is unable to do anything.

In my dictionary, laziness is a disease and If it is found, It should be treated as soon as possible but we have a habit of putting every work on tomorrow.

Now the question is,

If you are not thinking about yourself to break that laziness into work then who will do ?

And for why someone will do ?

He was deeply sad, looking around.

After some time, he just started to thinking..

If I work , If I don't show laziness in any work

What will happen ?

He take a mobile and started to writing in a note...

Every work will be on time.

There will be more focus on work.

I will be able to give time to myself and family.

I will start loving myself which will remove the tension. Everyone will be happy at home.

Financial condition will be so good.

I will become a good person in the eyes of other peoples.

There will be a self respect.

Life will be great.

But all this will happen If I remove the laziness from inside.

He started reading once again, what he has just typed.

He feels great, he decided to follow this and started taking an action.

There is a so much benefit and happiness by removing laziness from inside.

This will happen,

When I try...

Anyone can heal their life, If he/she wants to heal.

He decided to give a punishment to himself,

If he shows a laziness..

If I don't follow, I will give Rs. 500 to my enemy. (at least, we should not lie with ourselves) He started to work on himself but because of laziness, He has lost Rs.3500 but he was happy.

At least, he started working on himself.

Next few days, he lost more of money and it was going on...

After one month,

He was doing very well. He started working on small things and invested his valuable time in those things

He proudly says that I lost money but I am happy for that. When I started giving a punishment to myself,

I realised the value of money.

I realised the value of work.

I realised the value of respect.

I realised so many things, which we really don't think about.

We see around but we ignore it.

The every person,

The every place,

The every tree,

The every things...available on this planet giving us a big lessons but we are busy in other things.

Laziness will not change you, you change to laziness.

Most of us, thinking of past things which ruining your present and If the present is bad then how will be a better future ?

Please do think about it because This is your life.

ALWAYS REMEMBER

- Called a lazy person. How it feels ?

- Leave the laziness and start working.

- Laziness slowly destroys.

- Learn to give a punishment to yourself.

Question No - 27

Be lazy or be busy.

Please choose carefully,

After all, this is your life.

What will you choose and why ?

TWENTY-EIGHT

POSSIBLE

Everything is possible then why do we worry? Just do it and see the possibilities.

Everything is possible in this world.

If you dream it , you can achieve it because nothing is impossible.

If he/she can do it then Why can't I ?

I can also do.

If I put in my brain, nothing can stop me from achieving anything in the world.

What is stopping me ?

Do not take any support, nor any favour.

This world is yours and you have come to do

Something different in this world.

It does not matter whether you are white or black.

It does not matter, in which country you live.

Only one thing makes a difference is your thinking.

How you think to make that thing possible. It is in your hand.

Just believe in you and start working.

Forget the excuses and give a try.

It is a time to take an action.

Work hard.

Make a plan.

Just do it.

No one can stop me until I stop myself.

History can be created when you decide to make the history.

You just have to stay focused. You will find so many reasons for not doing a work.

You will get the peoples who will demotivate you by saying, you can not do. Look at you.

You are crazy but remember one thing, every person is a crazy for something and If he/she is not crazy then...how can they achieve it ?

How can they make a history ?

The day, when you start loving your work... from that day, work will start loving you.

The day, when you start working on your dream... from that day, dream start to help you to achieve your dream.

Everything is possible. When you think, it is possible.

Impossible, the word says itself..I am possible.

Believe in yourself and believe in your dream and make your dream possible.

ALWAYS REMEMBER

- Possible or Impossible is in our brain.

- You can think..you can make it.

- Nothing is impossible in this world.

- Give one more chance and see the possibilities.

Question No - 28

What is not possible for you ?

& Why ?

do you really think about it ?

TWENTY-NINE
UNSTOPPABLE

You can stop anything but your thinking is unstoppable.

Don't you like this ?

No one can stop me because I am unstoppable and no one can stop you because you are unstoppable.

I am unstoppable because I do what I love.

I am unstoppable because I believe in my dream.

I am unstoppable because I am going to get it.

I am unstoppable because I only focus on my path.

In this world,

If I can then definitely you can also. It can take time but you can also do it.

Here, we are talking about you. Alright.

Why are you unstoppable ?

No one can stop you in this world, unless you stop yourself.

You should be ready to become an unstoppable.

Once you have decided, nothing will stop you to keep going.

Your brain will stop working on the day, when you stop thinking.

When you stop reading.

When you stop eating.

As our body needs a food to work properly. Similarly, our brain also need some thoughts to work properly.

Your thinking has no limitations.

Until you stop thinking and when you stop thinking...you only stop yourself from improving.

You must be thankful that you are unstoppable.

In any situation, there is a solution but instead of solution...we always think about something else.

It does not take much time to destroy yourself and It does require more time, more patience, more hard work to have a better life.

We always have an options.

Either we should take a tension and always feel a stressful or live a life without tension.

I suggest, stay unstressed and keep moving in life to have a better experience in life.

Independent peoples never depend on anybody and other side, dependent peoples always expect something from others.

Which category, do you come ?

The dirtiest thing of our life is, we are expecting things instead of earning those things by respectfully.

Can't we earn ?

Of course, we can.

Nothing is impossible in this world.

Are you weak ?

Are you loser ?

Are you in debt ?

Don't you have a self respect ?

Don't you have a brain ?

Don't you think ?

Everyone knows,

How to walk? Then why are we walking behind someone else.

Why do we expect from others?

Do you deserve a life like this?

Have you imagined this type of life?

The day, when you stopped thinking about your life...that day will be the last day of your life because after that, you will live a life but in the eyes of others will be an identity of loser and in your eyes also the same.

Today, everything is possible.

Today is your day.

Today is something that can make your tomorrow better.

Tomorrow will come with new opportunities but for others.

You have only today and this is your day.

Make this day inspiring .

Make this day memorable.

ALWAYS REMEMBER

- Nothing can stop you to achieve. What you want to achieve.

- Enjoy the power of unstoppable.

- You are made for make things happen.

- Keep going.

Question No - 29

Can you just look at yourself ?

See..how lucky you are.

Your thinking is unstoppable but sadly, you are not thinking anything about yourself.

How sad it is!

THIRTY
FAITH

Little faith of someone's make you happy and your faith on your dream can make you more happy.

Faith is one thing which gives a motivation to do something different.

Faith is the one thing which gives a confidence to do something different.

Faith is the one thing which gives a visualisation to do something different.

Faith gives a visualisation in our mind that these are the things are happened and when we see that clear picture in our mind. We start working on to make that clear picture in reality.

Faith of, to be a successful.

Faith to make a dream come true.

Faith is the way of enjoying the life.

Our own faith makes a difference than others.

Are you enjoying that happiness?

Do you have confidence in your faith ?

If not,

You have to believe. You have no way.

How can you achieve a success? If you don't have a faith in you and your dream.

It is very important to have a faith in life to have a success or failure

It all starts with faith, believe.

Do you know the story of wilma rudolph ?

When wilma was born.

Dr. said, she will never walk in her life.

After hearing this,

Wilma's mother said,

She will walk.

She will run.

Rest is history.

1960 olympics, wilma rudolph won 3 gold and she is the first from america who won.

That was her mother faith that one day, she will walk and not she walked but she made a history in the world.

Everything is possible, when your faith is with you. When you believe in your faith.

Keep a faith and enjoy the life.

ALWAYS REMEMBER

- Faith in your dream.

- Faith of falling and rising.

- Faith is a hope that I can.

- Anything can happen with faith.

Question No - 30

Who will keep a faith on your dream ?

You or someone else...?

Why ?

If there is no faith, there is no hope.

THIRTY-ONE

THANK YOU

We all are thankful for something, for love, for support, for good lessons or even bad lessons of life.

I thank for everything.

You must thank for everything what you have got in your life.

You know why,

We are in profit actually, we came in this beautiful world without bringing anything and here after coming, we are getting so many things then why we are not happy ? Because we have forgotten to thank for what we have got.

I am thankful for my hair.

I am thankful for my eyes.

I am thankful for my face.

I am thankful for my ears.

I am thankful for my nose.

I am thankful for my hands.

I am thankful for my fingers.

I am thankful for my stomach.

I am thankful for my legs.

I am thankful for my body and I am thankful for each and every part of it.

There are so many peoples, who does not have some of those body parts but still they survive.

I am sure, you have everything.

I am thankful for those peoples, who did not tell me...what is right? Or what is wrong ?

If they told, I could not do so...

You should also...

I am thankful for each and every person who came in my life for giving me a good and bad experience to make me a better person.

You should be....

I am thankful for those peoples, who understand me because of that, I can understand someone else.

You should also...

I am thankful for those peoples, Who loves me for who am I ? and How I am ?

You should also...

I am thankful for those peoples, who gives

Me their valuable time.

You should also....

I am thankful for those peoples, who supports me.

I am thankful for every moment that taught me to live.

I am thankful for the bad time that taught me to get up.

I am thankful for keeping me positive so that

I can spread positivity.

I am thankful for making me kind so that I can spread kindness.

I am thankful for making me mad so that I am behind my love.

I am thankful for every person for everything for teaching me something in life.

And of course, I am very very thankful to my family because they never ask me that what am I doing ?

I think, They believe...LOTS OF LOVE.

ALWAYS REMEMBER

- Thank for everything what you have.

- There are so many people who wants to live a life like you living.

- Thank for those, who gave a good and bad experience.

- Always Be thankful.

" Think About It "

The truth is still ignored,

Everyday, more than 200000 peoples died naturally in the world.

Are you still alive ?

Don't you think that you are a lucky one that you are alive today.

Thank you for another day.

Nitesh More

Author of 3 Life changing books called " Feel the change", " Super 31 " and Marathi Book " Jivan Jivan Aahe ka ? "

Currently, He is working as an Assistant Director and a Script Writer in the Indian Film and Television Industry.

He has written, Directed and Produced a Hindi Short Film Called " BASURI-The flute" and a script writer of Marathi Short film " NAKKI CHUK KONACHI ? "

He has directed a Marathi Ahirani song called " MANA DILVAR KAYA RE VAAR "

Studied from Night college, Mumbai. He loves watching a movies, Writing, reading a books, Playing a cricket and travelling.

जीवन
जीवन
आहे
का ?
नितेश मोरे

" Inspirational, Life Changing Book "

Feel The Change

Thank you so much for your love and support. It means a LOT to me.

9 798887 041858

Printed by Libri Plureos GmbH in Hamburg,
Germany